© 1994 Watts Books

Watts Books
96 Leonard Street
London
EC2A 4RH

Franklin Watts Australia
14 Mars Road
Lane Cove
NSW 2066

UK ISBN: 0 7496 1532 X

Dewey Decimal Classification Number 387.7

10 9 8 7 6 5 4 3 2 1

A CIP catalogue record for this book is available from the British Library.

Editor: Sarah Ridley
Designer: Janet Watson
Picture researcher: Sarah Moule
Illustrators: Robert and Rhoda Burns

Photographs: Chris Fairclough Colour Library 6; BAA Heathrow 15; Eye Ubiquitous 16, 26b; Image Bank 26t; Robert Harding Picture Library 21; Telegraph Colour Library cover; Tony Stone Worldwide 11, 12, 23, 24, 28; ZEFA 9, 18.

Printed in Malaysia

LIFT OFF!

AIRPORTS

Joy Richardson

WATTS BOOKS
London • New York • Sydney

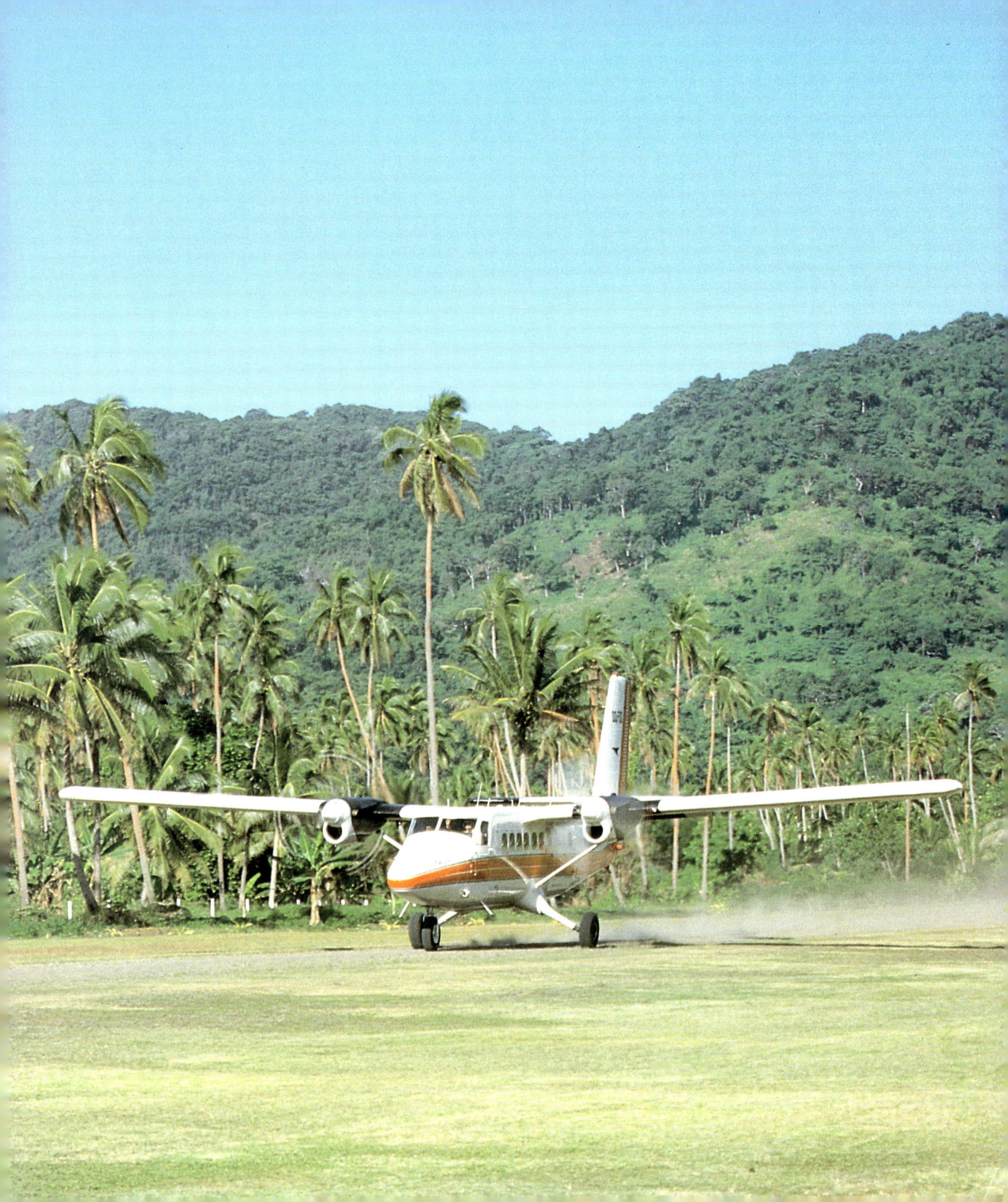

Early airports

The first aeroplanes took off
and landed on grassy fields.
The planes were small and light
and only carried a few passengers.
Airports were hardly needed.

Nowadays, huge aeroplanes carry
hundreds of passengers at a time.
Each year, hundreds of millions
of people travel by air.

Airports have been built to organise
all this air travel and keep it safe.
Some airports are quite small but
many are large and very busy.

Planning the space

A large airport may cover as much space as a whole town.

It must be planned very carefully to provide long runways and to make life easy for passengers.

From high above the airport you can see the layout of runways, roads, buildings and parking spaces. Each airport has its own design, but they all have the same job to do.

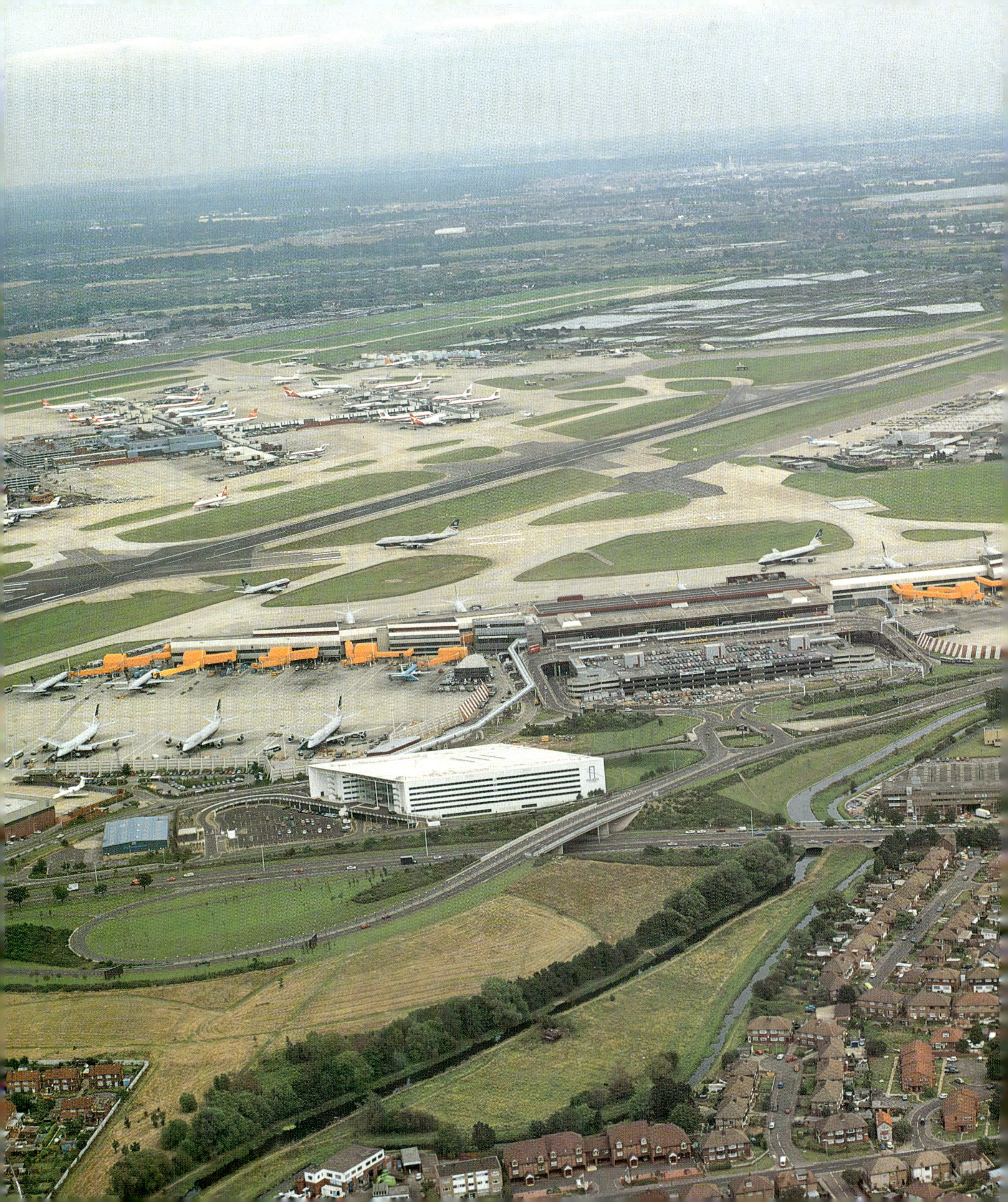

The terminal building

At the heart of the airport is the terminal building. Here passengers start and finish their journey.

Different airlines have desks where they check tickets and collect baggage for each flight.

Passengers can go shopping or eat a meal in the terminal building.

Indicator boards show the times of planes arriving and departing.

Some airports have several terminals.

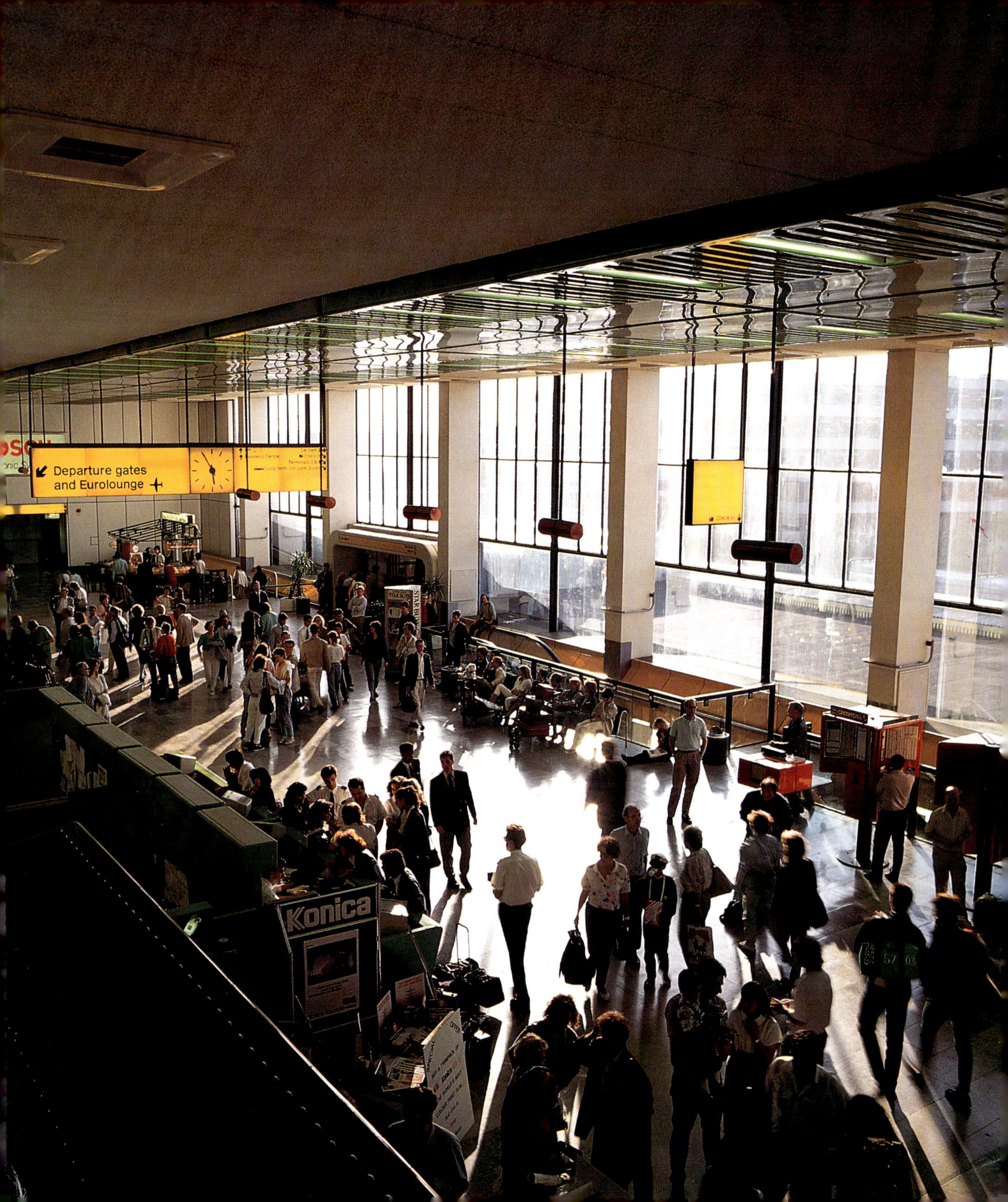

Departure gates
and Eurolounge
Konica

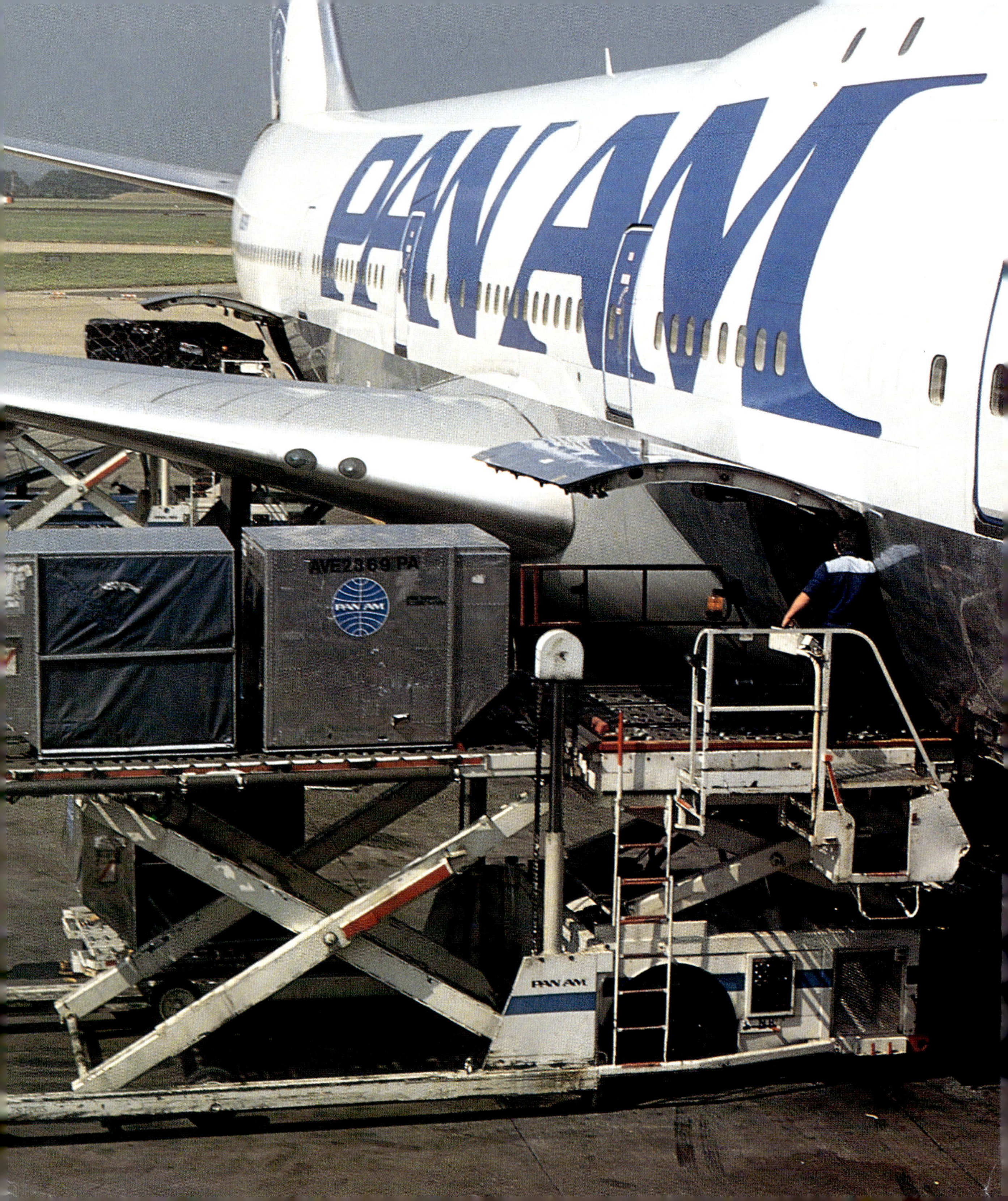
PAN AM
AVE2369 PA
PAN AM
PAN AM

Handling the baggage

Bags and suitcases are weighed, labelled and taken away on a conveyor belt.

Behind the scenes, the baggage is sorted onto wagons which are towed out to the plane.

The baggage is loaded into the cargo hold in the bottom of the plane. Huge containers or even cars may also be lifted into the hold.

The cargo may weigh many tonnes, but it must be evenly spread to keep the plane level.

Keeping safe

Airports take great care to keep people safe.

Passengers may have to walk through a metal detector.

Hand baggage is X-rayed to make sure it contains no weapons.

Passports are checked to watch out for criminals.

Fire engines and ambulances are kept ready for emergencies.

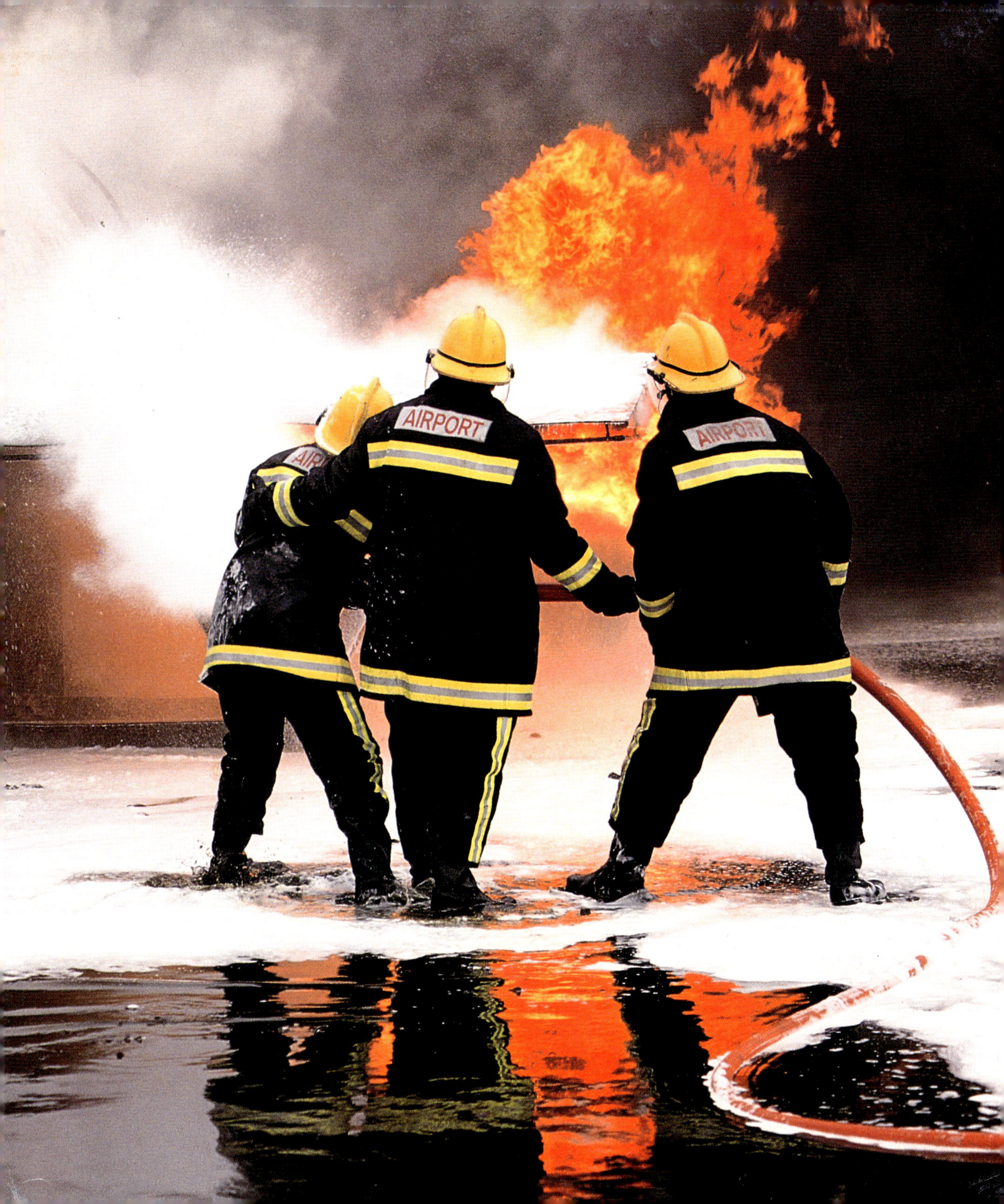
AIRPORT
AIRPORT

Cessna
ENG.
ENG.
CESSNA
MODELS
310F
310G
310H
310I
310J
310K
SERVICE MANUAL

Getting ready

Planes wait on the area around the terminal building called the apron.

There are lots of jobs to be done quickly before the next flight.

Engineers check the engines and all the controls to make sure everything is working properly.

Fuel is brought to the plane by tankers or underground pipes.

The plane is cleaned and new supplies are taken on board.

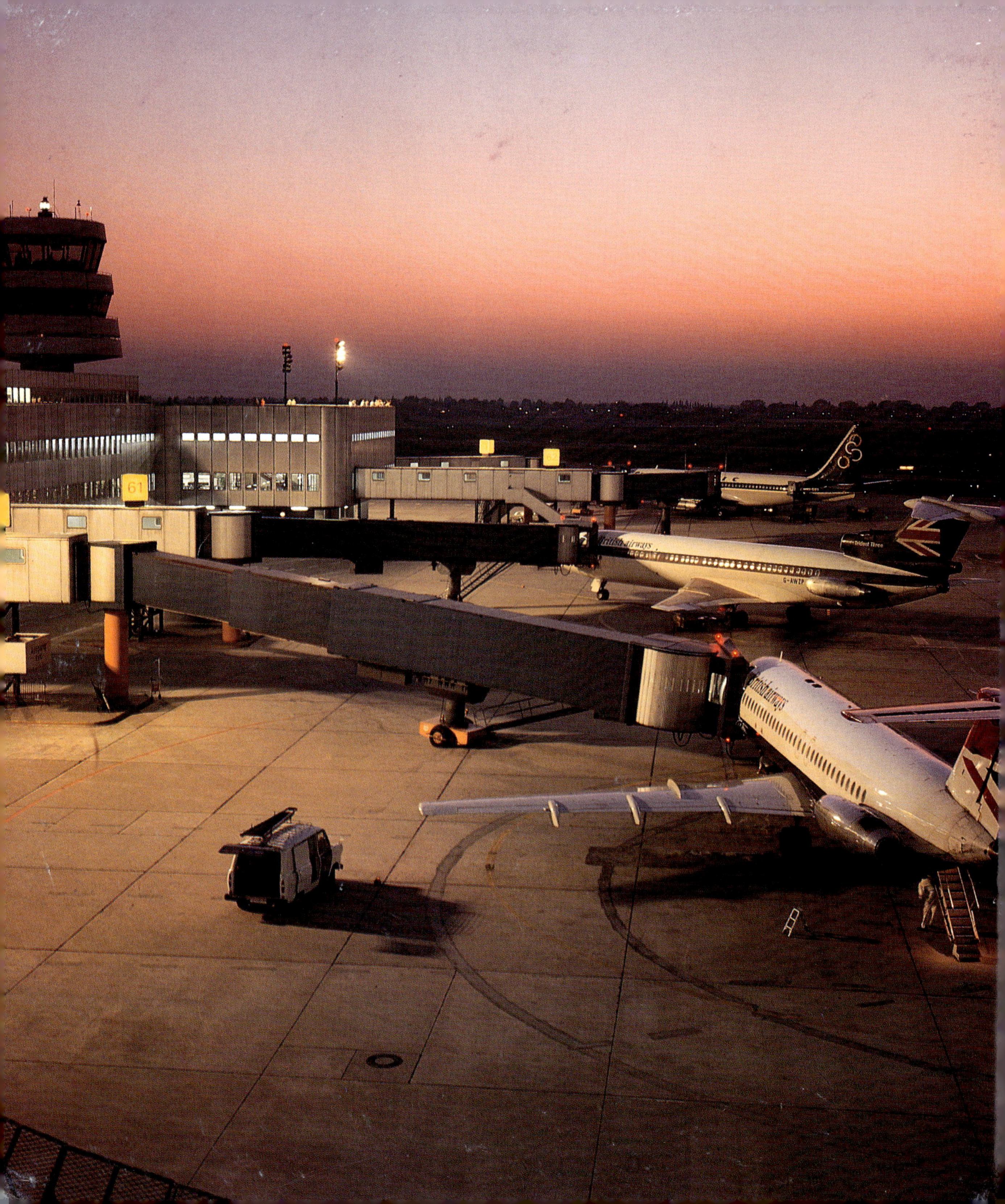
61

All aboard

Passengers wait in the departure lounge until their plane is ready for them.

Then they are called to board the plane from one of the exits called gates.

A covered passageway sticks out from the building to the door of the plane.

At some airports passengers walk out to the plane or take a ride on a bus.

When everyone is ready and the doors are closed, the engines start.

A special tractor called a tug tows the plane out of its parking space.

Down the runway

The plane moves slowly along linking roads called taxiways to the start of the runway.

Long straight runways are needed for taking off and landing. Runways have a flat, smooth surface of concrete or tarmac.

The largest runways are over three kilometres long and as wide as a motorway.

Runway

Taxiway

NO SMOKING
ATTEND
RAIN REPELLENT
TAXI
APU
FLAP
PARKING BRAKE PULL
CUTOFF
FLAP DOWN
STAB TRIM

Keeping control

At busy airports there may be a plane taking off every minute and another plane coming in to land. This takes a lot of organising.

Ground controllers look out over the whole airport from the top of a tall control tower.

They control all the movements of aircraft on the ground. They tell pilots when to take off.

Approach controllers watch arriving planes on radar screens and tell them when to land.

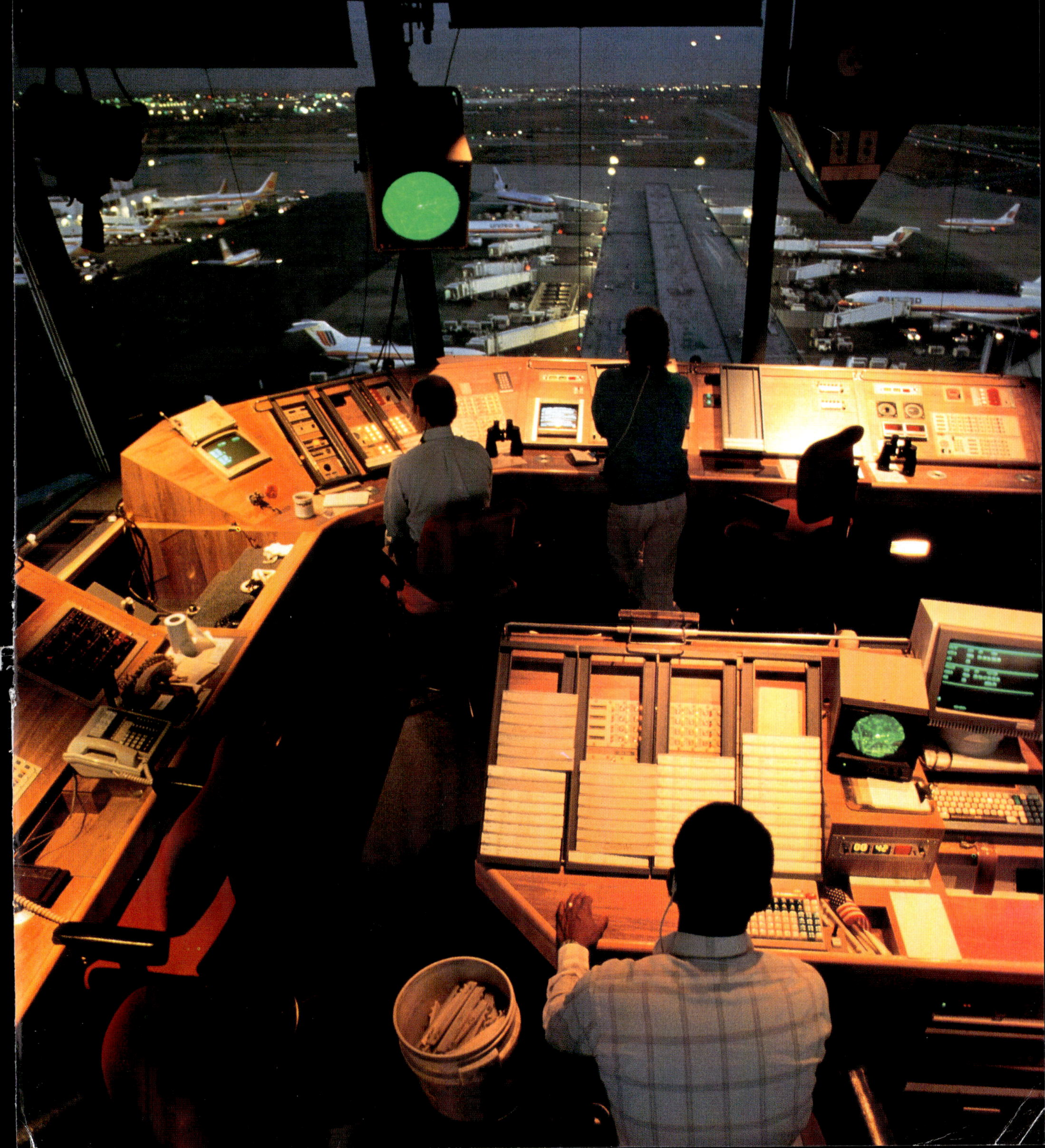

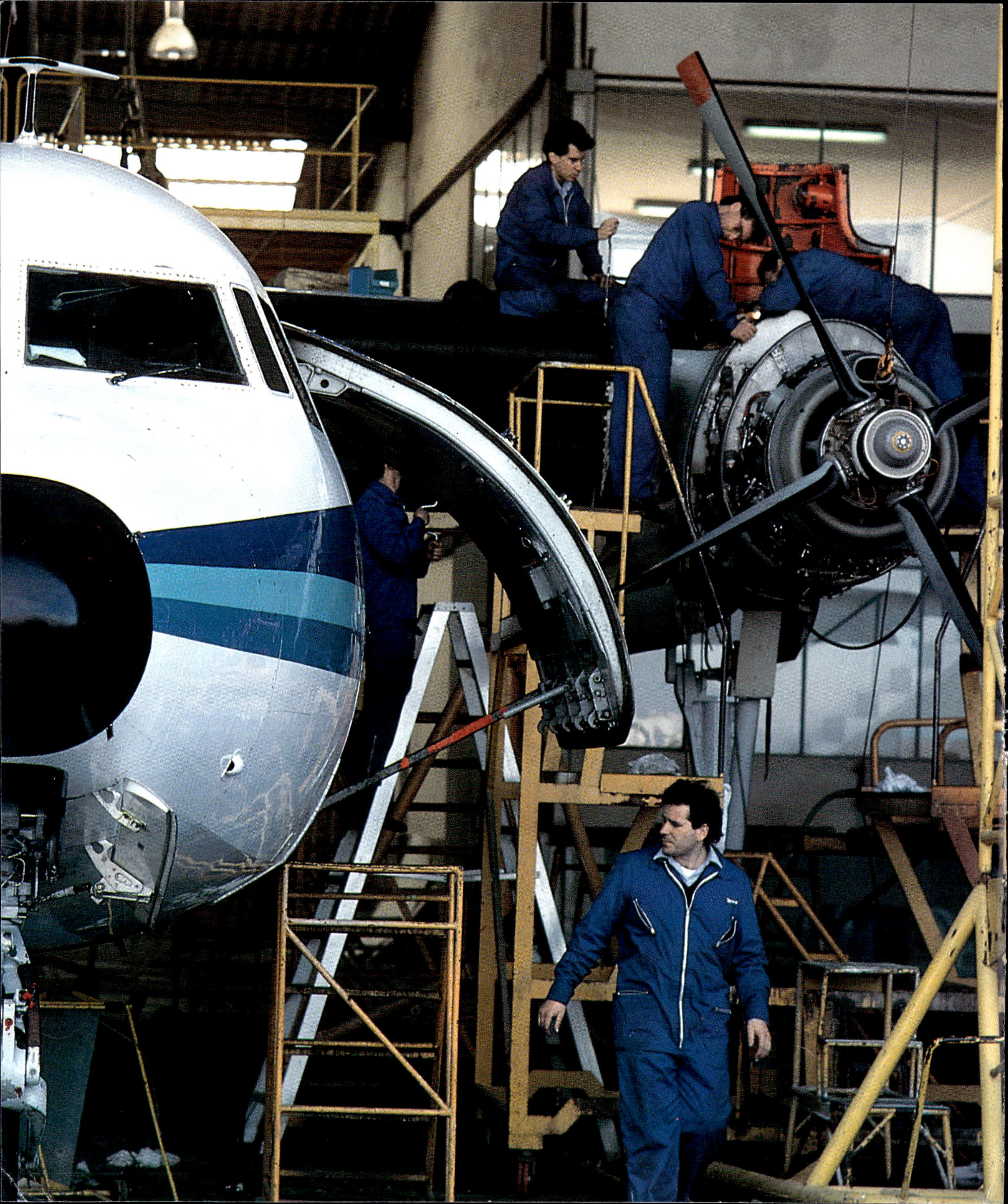

Engineers at work

As planes roar into the sky, lots of other work goes on around the airport.

Every plane must be serviced regularly to keep it safe for flying.

Away from the runways there are giant hangars where engineers clean and repair the planes and replace old parts.

They use X-ray machines to search for cracks in the metal. They strip down the engines and carry out tests on every part of the plane.

MAERSK
CITYFLYER

Spectators
Emergency exit
VILLAGE
Emergency exit

Journey's end

At the end of their journey,
passengers arrive at another airport.

It may be bigger or smaller
than the one they left from,
but it will also have a runway,
a control tower and a terminal building.

Controllers guide the plane in to land.
Baggage handlers unload the luggage.

Cars and buses, trains and taxis
wait to carry people away.

Every airport is a doorway into
another city or another country.

Airport facts

Sixty million passengers a year pass through Chicago O'Hare, the busiest airport in the world.

King Khalid airport in Saudi Arabia is the largest in the world. It covers an area of 225 square kilometres.

London Heathrow has the most passengers flying between different countries and it is used by the most airlines.

Index

Apron 17

Baggage handling 13
Boarding the plane 19

Cargo 13
Check-in desks 10
Chicago O'Hare 28
Control towers 22
Crime 14

Departure lounges 19

Emergencies 14

Gates 19
Ground controllers 22

Hangars 25

Indicator boards 10

King Khalid airport 28

London Heathrow 28

Metal detectors 14

Passports 14

Refuelling 17
Routine checks 17
Runways 20

Safety 14

Taking off and landing 22
Taxiways 20
Terminal buildings 10

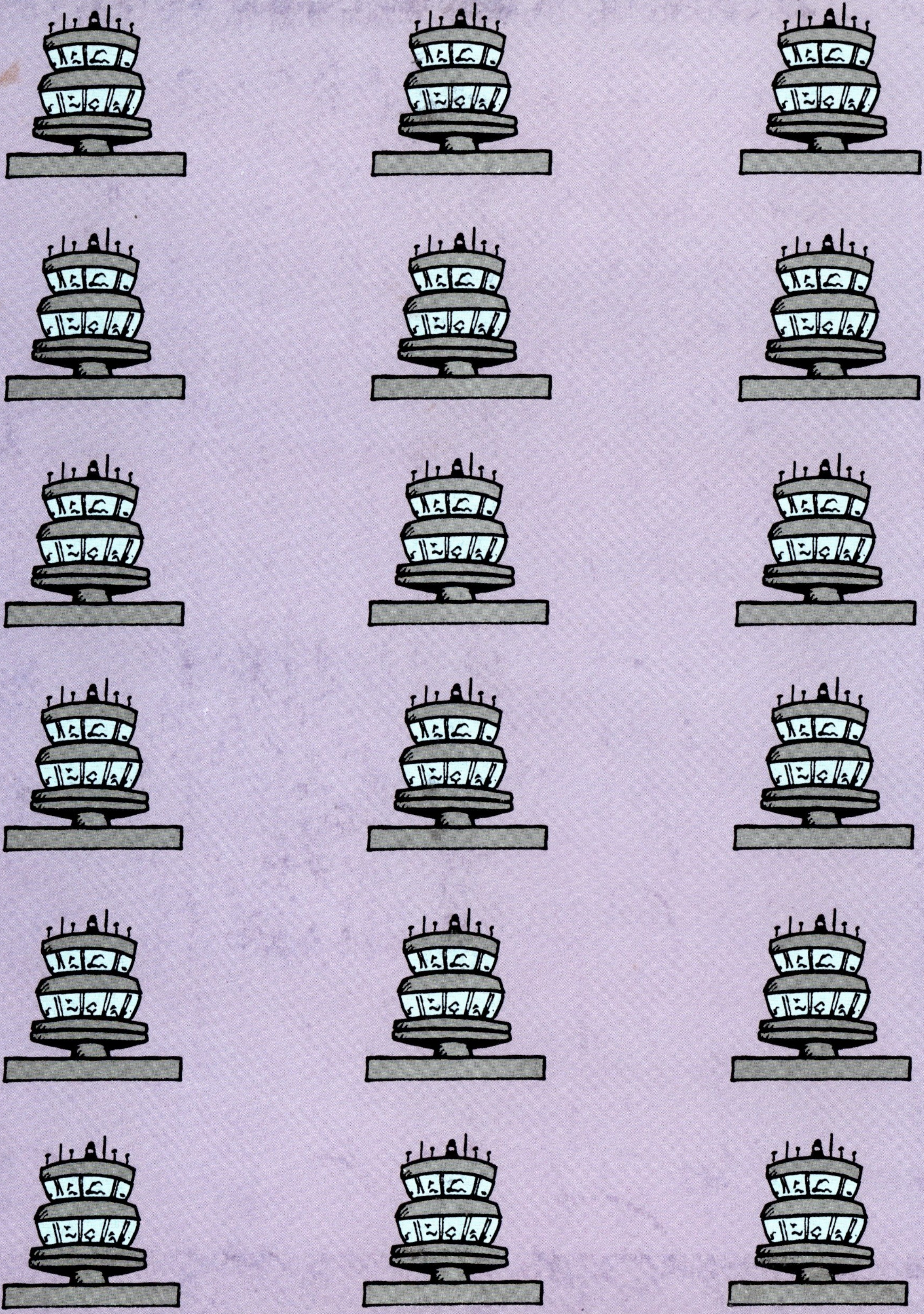